Contents

Name: _______________________________

1 Design a cover for your handwriting folder

Set out a Title box. Write your name and year carefully.
Practise different patterns in the two boxes.

Name ____________________

Year ____________________

Handwriting patterns

2 A personal fact sheet

Use these questions to help you design your own personal fact sheet that you will keep in the front of your handwriting folder.

My name is ___________________________

I am ___________ years old.

I am in Year ___________

My hair is ___________ and my eyes are

____

I am ___________ tall.

My teacher's name is ___________

I am good at ___________

____

____

____

____

I find it very hard to ___________

____

____

So far, my handwriting is (tick a circle):

Brilliant! ◯   OK ◯   I need more practice. ◯

3 My likes and dislikes

Now write out a personal fact sheet about your likes and dislikes.
Keep this fact sheet in the front of your handwriting folder.

My favourite meal is ___________________________

____

The clothes I like wearing best are ______________

____

The team I support is ____________________________

____

On TV, I like to watch __________________________

____

I love ____

____

I hate ____

____

____

I wish I could __________________________________

____

____

My handwriting:
A checklist

In this book, most of your handwriting will be in a joined style.
It is time to think about how well you are progressing.
Use this sheet to think about your handwriting.

Materials

Is your pen/pencil comfortable?	Yes No
Do you have enough room to write?	Yes No
Can you tilt your sheet of paper?	Yes No

Presentation

Can someone else read your writing?	Yes No
Does it look neat?	Yes No
Do all your headings and titles stand out clearly?	Yes No

Style

Are all the letters of the correct size?	Yes No
Is the shape of each letter clear?	Yes No
Are all the letters formed correctly?	Yes No
Are all the lower case letters joined?	Yes No
Do they all slant in the same direction?	Yes No
Are any letters too cramped?	Yes No
Do some letters or joins need more practice?	Yes No
If yes, which are they?	

____

____

____

Letter joins

ai ar un

Write each word as many times as you can on one line.

> *chair heart funny maiden smart stun*
> *daisy chart blunder wait party thunder*

Write all the **ai** words in alphabetical order.

____

____

____

____

Write all the **ar** words in alphabetical order.

____

____

____

____

Write all the **un** words in alphabetical order.

____

____

____

____

er ir ur

Write each word as many times as you can on one line.

> her stir turn herd bird turnip perch
> quirk future mother birth fur

Write all the **er** words in alphabetical order.

Write all the **ir** words in alphabetical order.

Write all the **ur** words in alphabetical order.

7 Letter joins

air are

Write each word as many times as you can on one line.

> *hair dare fair hare pair scare chair*
> *square stair stare dairy bare*

Write all the *air* words in alphabetical order.

____

____

____

____

____

Write all the *are* words in alphabetical order.

____

____

____

____

____

8 Letter joins

aer eir ear

Write each word as many times as you can on one line.

> aerial heir pear aerosol their bear
> aeroplane tear aerodynamics fearsome

Write all the *aer* words in alphabetical order.

Write all the *eir* words in alphabetical order.

Write all the *ear* words in alphabetical order.

Letter joins

ore oor

Write each word as many times as you can on one line.

> *sore door more floor score moor store*
> *spoor before poor explore boorish*

Write all the *ore* words in alphabetical order.

____

____

____

____

____

Write all the *oor* words in alphabetical order.

____

____

____

____

____

Handwriting check 1:
"On the vowels – a riddle"

Write this poem in your best handwriting.
Can you solve the riddle?

We are airy little creatures,
All of different voice and features;
One of us in glass is set,
One of us you'll find in jet,
T'other you may see in tin
And the fourth a box within;
If the fifth you should pursue,
It can never fly from you.

Jonathon Swift

Punctuation:
"Stig of the Dump"

Copy this passage in your best handwriting,
inserting the correct punctuation.

Think carefully about which words should
have a capital letter at the beginning.
Some of the writing is in speech.
How will you show this?

something or somebody had a lot of shaggy black
hair and two bright black eyes that were looking
very hard at barney
hullo said barney
something said nothing
i fell down the cliff said barney
somebody grunted
my names barney
somebody something made a noise that sounded
like stig

Story beginnings

These phrases will be useful when you want to begin a story.
Write them carefully and keep them in your Handwriting folder.

Once upon a time ...

One dark and stormy night ...

The other day ...

It all began when ...

It would never have happened if ...

Now write a story beginning of your own, using one of the phrases
listed above.

13 Story endings

These phrases will be useful when you want to end a story.
Write them carefully and keep them in your Handwriting folder.

And they all lived happily ever after.

... and he was never seen in that town again.

And from that day to this ...

So it all ended with ...

The battle was won and my tale is done.

... but after all, it was only a dream.

Read the letter below and use it to help you write your own thank-you letter. Use a set of guidelines, if you wish.

Think about this!

When we receive a special present, it is thoughtful to write a thank-you letter.
Do you know the rhyme that the presents mentioned in the letter below come from?

Tiny Cottage,
Field Lane,
Springtown
January 5th

Dear Mr Stevenson,

Thank you so much for all the presents you sent me for Christmas. I have planted the pear tree in my orchard and the partridge is nesting happily. The turtle doves are up in the dovecote and their cooing continues both day and night, scattering the French hens every time they settle. The four calling birds have got their legs trapped in the gold rings and the six geese have trampled up my lawn, along with eight cows. (The swans are somewhat large for my water feature!)
Last night at supper, I was entertained by your nine fiddlers. It is a pity they only know one tune, but at least the ten drummers kept a steady beat and the dancing ladies seemed not to mind. I wonder what you will expect me to do with twelve lords? This is to let you know that I am shortly emigrating to Australia and so will not be here for another Christmas.

Yours thankfully,
Miss M. Bulstrode

Don't forget to date your work!

Practise writing these dates in different styles of presentation.

Some words below have been abbreviated. How do you indicate an abbreviation?
You may write some of the dates in joined handwriting and some in print.
Do you know what is special about the date in number 4?

Miss Bulstrode dated
her letter like this: January 5th

She could have
written it like this: Jan. 5th 1896
or like this: 5/1/96

She could have
added the day: Tuesday January 5th 1896

How did you write today's date in school?

Try writing these dates in different styles:

1. 21/3/1997

2. Thursday 15th August 1794

3. Wed. 23rd October

4. Tues. 29th Feb. 2000

5. Sunday the twenty-third of November, 1903

Silent letters

k w g

Practise writing all of the words in the box in alphabetical order.
Write each word as many times as you can on one line.

knight write gnaw knock wring gnome
knee wreck gnarled knick-knack wrought
gnash knife wrap gnat

Silent letters

h

Practise writing all of the words in the box in alphabetical order.
Write each word as many times as you can on one line.

> ghost rhino gherkin what ghastly
> rhyme rhubarb ghoul rhythm when
> rhapsody which bhaji thyme

Silent letters

b t

Practise writing all of the words in the box in alphabetical order.
Write each word as many times as you can on one line.

> bomb often dumb castle debt
> whistle crumb wrestle limb soften
> plumber thistle tomb listen comb

Double letters

tt   mm

Practise writing all of the words in the box in alphabetical order.
Write each word as many times as you can on one line.

pretty   hammer   little   summer   kettle
swimmer   bottle   humming   skittle   slimmer
rattle   dimmer   cottage   jammed   attic

Double letters

dd bb

Practise writing all of the words in the box in alphabetical order.
Write each word as many times as you can on one line.

> saddle   hobble   middle   rabbit   muddle
> dribble   paddle   bubble   fiddle   wobble
> ribbed   studded   huddle   fibbed   waddle

Double letters

bb tt dd gg pp zz

Practise writing all of the words in the box in alphabetical order.
Write each word as many times as you can on one line.

struggle battle ripple babble guzzle
meddle dazzle scuttle frazzle fizzle giggle
wiggle scatter puddle dropped

Handwriting check 2:
Silly sentences

Practise double letters by writing these silly sentences
in your best handwriting.

Think about this! Write each sentence once. Then try to write it as quickly as you can without spoiling your handwriting. You might make up another silly double-letter sentence for your partner to try.

Betty Ritter potted butter.

Jammy James dribbled jam on his jim-jams.

Jenny plucked the strings in the middle of her fiddle.

ou vi wi

Practise writing the words in the box in alphabetical order.

Think about this!

To help you remember these words, practise writing each one at least five times.
Remember to Look, Say, Cover, Write and Check!
Try not to lift your pencil off the paper until you have finished writing a whole word.
When you have finished, place your pencil on the line and try writing each word again with your eyes closed.

> shout vile wiggle about visitor wisdom
> route vital window detour violin width

Handwriting check 3:
"Higgledy-Piggledy"

Write this poem in your best handwriting.

You could enlarge, *italicise* or <u>underline</u> some words to help someone read them aloud and make the poem more dramatic.

Why do you think the author used brackets for the final two lines?

Higgledy-Piggledy
keeps his room tidy.
He fluffs up his pillows
And smooths down his spread.
He straightens out drawers
And he dusts every corner.

(Just wait till I dump
All my trash on his bed!)

Myra Cohn Livingston

Some words you should know

Write the words in the box in alphabetical order. Write each word as many times as you can on one line. Practise reading the words aloud with your partner.

vowel   alphabet   onset   rime   antonym
synonym   syllable   analogy   phoneme   suffix
letter   calligram   homonym   consonant

Prefixes

un dis

Add the prefixes to the words in the box. Do any of the words take both prefixes? Write each new word as many times as you can on one line. Continue your work on another sheet of paper.

> happy appointed sure satisfied opened applied fortunate interested affected able inclined do may

Prefixes

de re

Add the prefixes to the words in the box. Do any of the words take both prefixes? Write each new word in alphabetical order, as many times as you can on one line.

bug pair face act assure lay light collect fine cover action hydrate

28 Prefixes

Add the prefixes to the words in the box.
Write each new word as many times as you can on one line.
Continue your work on another sheet of paper.

fix sent pare tend serve historic
destine paid view dispose tender
vent judge mature

Some words you should know

Write the words in the box in alphabetical order. Write each word as many times as you can on one line. Practise reading the words aloud with your partner.

tongue-twister myth sequel fable riddle legend poem sequence ode story limerick tale dialogue parable

Some words you should know

Write the words in the box in alphabetical order. Write each word as many times as you can on one line. Practise reading the words aloud with your partner.

> noun exclamation suffix adverb verb syntax
> punctuation conjunction question pronoun
> prefix adjective grammar preposition

Letter joins

ab ul it

Practise writing the words in the box in alphabetical order.

Think about this!

To help you remember these words, practise writing each one at least five times.
Remember to Look, Say, Cover, Write and Check!
Try not to lift your pencil off the paper until you have finished writing a whole word.
When you have finished, place your pencil on the line and try writing each word again with your eyes closed.

fable hopeful kitchen disable sullen kitten crab seagull fritter habit full bitter

Prefixes

mis non

Add the prefixes to the words in the box. Do any of the words take both prefixes? Write each new word as many times as you can on one line. Continue your work on another sheet of paper.

take existent handle stop guided committal entity adventure stick fit conduct sense behave event chief

Prefixes

ex co

Add the prefixes to the words in the box. Do any of the words take both prefixes? Write each new word as many times as you can on one line. Continue your work on another sheet of paper.

> *it operate tend habit hale exist ample at efficient change incidence claim vet act port*

anti

Add the prefix to the words in the box, writing the new words in alphabetical order. Use a dictionary to check whether a hyphen is used in each new word.

> perspirant body social clockwise freeze
> septic biotic tetanus hero climax
> static cyclone lock matter dote

Writing a shape poem:
"The Squirmy Worm"

Write this poem and then decorate it with suitable illustrations.

Think about this!

"The Squirmy Worm" is a shape poem. The words have been set out in the shape of a worm. How would you set out a poem about a snail, or a snake? You could even compose a shape poem of your own.

I can wiggle wriggle squirt through dirt then hump

stretch sky the at peek jump bump

far far down into earth curl and furl twirl and swirl about then push up up up whirl around

down deep deep way way dive again again cause I'm a squirmy worm— that's why!

Pamela Mordecai

Join the syllables

Using a syllable from each line in the box, make nine whole words.
Underline the vowels in each word you make.

> good pic son house gar win work up nap
> clock kid Sam lift dow night den nic light

Think about this! Find some more two-syllable words and write them on this page. Write each syllable on a small piece of card or paper. Jumble them up. Now play a game of match-the-syllables with your partner or a friend.

Join the syllables

Using a syllable from each line in the box, make nine whole words.
Underline the vowels in each word you make.

cliff bung oct mast hist but ex voll mocc
er ey or a er hang a ter o
cup cise ful ic er ball pus low sin

____

____

____

____

____

____

____

____

____

Think about this! Find some more three-syllable words and write them on this page. Write each syllable on a small piece of card or paper. Jumble them up. Now play a game of match-the-syllables with your partner or a friend.

ol wh ot

Practise writing the words in the box in alphabetical order.

Think about this!

To help you remember these words, practise writing each one at least five times.
Remember to Look, Say, Cover, Write and Check!
Try not to lift your pencil off the paper until you have finished writing a whole word.
When you have finished, place your pencil on the line and try writing each word again with your eyes closed.

old what rotten soldier when hot-pot holiday who spotty folding where slot

Suffixes

ful ly

Add the suffixes to the words in the box. Do any of the words take both suffixes? Write each new word as many times as you can on one line. Continue your work on another sheet of paper.

> pain quick help smooth sorrow rough grate
> excited joy slow bash late hope wise

less

Add the suffix to the words in the box, writing the new words in alphabetical order. Write each word as many times as you can on one line.

hope end thank clue speech feature care fear pain smoke sight tire harm sense help

Handwriting check 4:
"The Cockatoo"

Write this poem in your best handwriting.

The Cockatoo is
widely known
For talking on the
telephone
And also (wretched,
thoughtless bird)
For hanging up with
out a word.

John Gardner

Think about this!

"Thoughtless" means: without thought.
Use this example to write a definition for each
of the following words: "helpless", "hopeless", "painless",
"clueless", "hairless".

Number-words

Write the number-words in the box in numerical order.
Write each number-word as many times as you can on the line.

fiftieth forty-fourth sixth fourth fifty-second
thirty-fifth second fortieth thirteenth
first tenth ninety-ninth twenty-first

Around the world

Write the country names in the box in alphabetical order.

Use an atlas to find the names of some more countries to write in joined handwriting.
You might make a poster with each country's name next to an illustration of its national flag.

New Zealand Wales Bangladesh Zimbabwe Scotland Australia India Pakistan Japan Chile Iraq Denmark Mauritius Mauritania

44 Writing labels

Write each country name in the box inside the correct outline shape.

Think about this!

Sometimes, labels are more clear if they are written in print. You may choose to write some or all of your labels in print. Use an atlas if you need to.

Germany   France   Spain   Italy

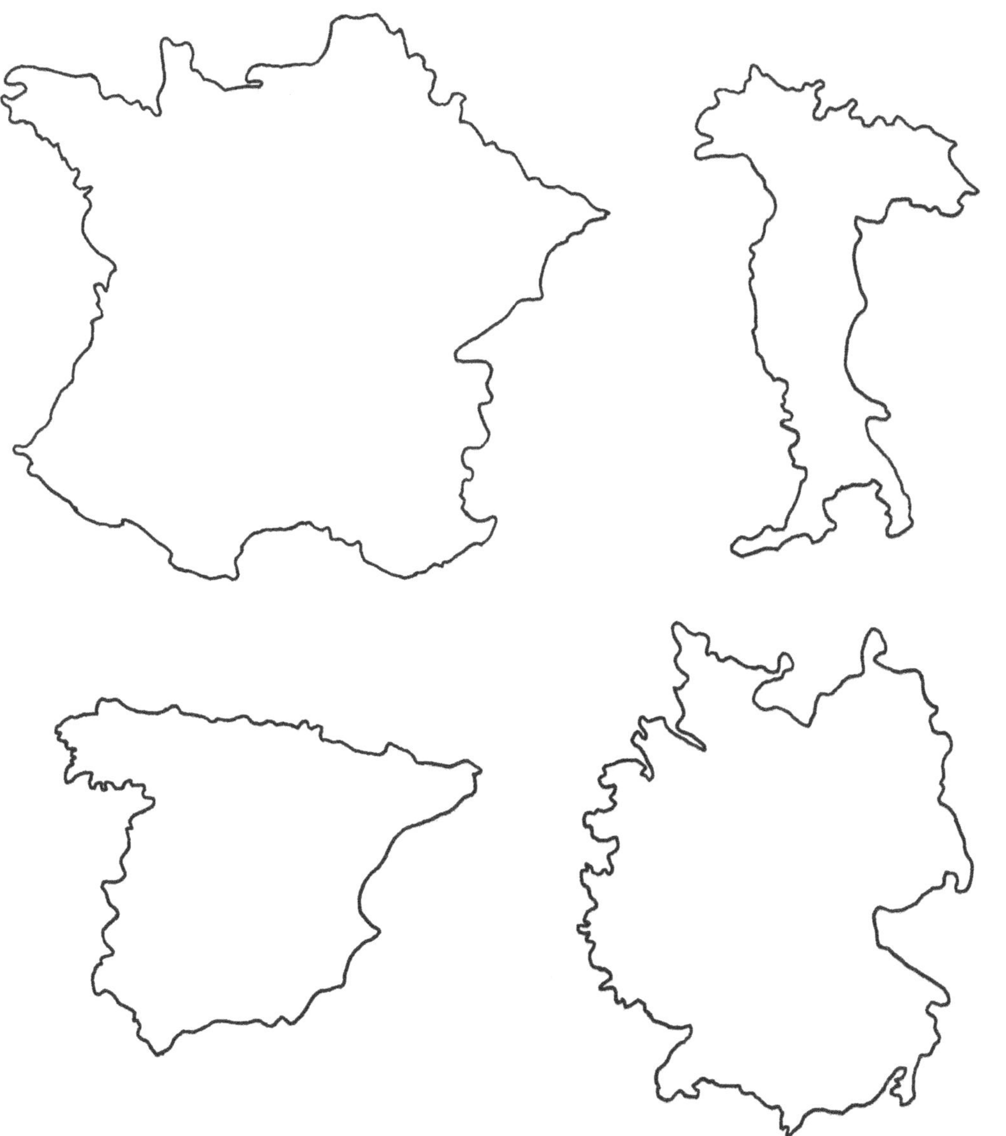

A favourite poem or rhyme

Choose a poem or rhyme and write it in your best handwriting.

Think about this!

Don't choose a poem or rhyme that is too long or it might not fit on the page.
You might keep your poem or rhyme a secret to share later with your partner or friends.
You can illustrate or decorate your poem or rhyme, if you wish.

How well do you write at speed?

In activity 45, you were asked to use your best handwriting.
Go back to the checklist (sheet number 4) to assess how well
you are progressing. Best handwriting takes a lot of time and care
to produce. Sometimes you need to write very quickly.
On the lines below, write as much as you can about your
best friend in two minutes. You may need to use a clock or timer.

Check your speed writing

Use the questions below to help you think about your speed writing.

<u>Speed writing and making notes</u>

Do you use joined writing to make notes?   Yes   No

Can you read your own notes, later?   Yes   No

Is your handwriting still readable when you write quickly?   Yes   No

Did you need to stop in the middle of a word to think how to join any letters?   Yes   No

If yes, which letters were they?

____

____

____

____

Can your best friend read your speed writing?   Yes   No

Do you like your handwriting?   Yes   No

What do you need to practise next?

____

____

____

____